TIME MACHINE
The Story of H. G. Wells

World Writers

TIME MACHINE
The Story of H. G. Wells

William J. Boerst

MORGAN
REYNOLDS
Incorporated

Greensboro

TIME MACHINE *The Story of H. G. Wells*

Photo credits: University of Illinois Library at Urbana-Champaign

Library of Congress Cataloging-in-Publication Data

Boerst, William J.
    Time Machine : the Story of H. G. Wells / William J. Boerst. -- 1st
ed.
            p.   cm. -- (World Writers)
    Includes bibliographical references and index.
    Summary: Explores the personal life and literary career of the
wide-ranging British author known for his science fiction,
histories, and novels.
    ISBN 1-883846-40-4
    1. Wells, H. G. (Herbert George), 1866-1946 Juvenile literature.
2. Wells, H. G. (Herbert George), 1866-1946--Political and social
views Juvenile literature. 3. Novelists, English--20th century
Biography Juvenile literature. 4. Science fiction, English--History
and criticism Juvenile literature. [1. Wells, H. G. (Herbert
George), 1866-1946. 2. Authors, English.] I. Title. II. Series.
PR5776.B58   2000
823' .912--dc21
[B]

99-41832
CIP

Printed in the United States of America
First Edition

*With Love
to Rae*

CONTENTS

H. G. Wells

Chapter One

Humble Beginnings

H. G. Wells had many ideas about how to change a great number of things. One of the things he most wanted to change was the way children were educated. He based many of his ideas about education on his own experiences. He remembered entering a school in his hometown of Bromley, England, at age seven in 1873. The teacher, Mr. Morley, was bald and wore glasses. His nose was always red and he sported gray whiskers. His discipline took the form of corporal punishment using his hands, a cane, books, or rulers. Students sometimes had to stand on desks and hold books or slates away from their bodies until their arms ached. The class numbered twenty-five to thirty-five students, ages seven to fifteen. Half were boarders; the other half were children from poor and middle-class families nearby. Class sessions lasted from nine till twelve and from two till five.

Usually Mr. Morley sat in a distant manner, removed from the trials of the classroom. Bertie later recalled how students spent their time: "...we used to draw on our slates, tell one another fantastic stories, trade in stamps, play games with marbles, eat sweets and tarts, and bread and butter, while the process of our education was in active progress." When Morley fell asleep, the boys would make weird faces or creep around the room. Startled, Morley would wake, punish those he had caught, and spend the next hour driving the boys ruthlessly in drill work. When he was upset, Morley's breathing became labored and he ground his teeth together. The boys heard colorful name-calling from his lips: "miserable wobblers...sniveling chumplepumpennies...wiggle waggle...hound."

As an adult H.G. had trouble remembering what he had learned in Morley's classroom. "I do not remember any teaching at all at school.... our loss was chiefly negative—we grew up dull." What he didn't learn at school, Bertie picked up from the Bromley Literary Institute, which was the local library, or his father's book collection at home.

Bertie's father, Joseph, and mother, Sarah, tried to make a living by selling china, glassware, and later, cricket supplies. But business was not good and they never seemed to escape poverty. The crockery shop was on the ground floor of their row house. The family took their meals, usually potatoes and cabbage, in the basement kitchen. Bertie could look out the only window at the feet of people passing on the outside grating. One steep, twisting staircase led up to the shop and another to the family's bedrooms on the top floor.

Bertie's small backyard looked out into a neighborhood of hardship and hard work. On one side the neighboring butcher kept pigs, sheep, and cattle awaiting slaughter. On killing day

Bertie and his family lived on busy Bromley Street while he was a boy.

Bertie listened to the animals' final cries and screams. Beyond this was the churchyard where Bertie's sister lay buried. Another neighbor was a haberdasher (seller of hats) who grew mushrooms and used horse manure as fertilizer. A tailor and his helpers sewed in a workroom on the other side. Bertie's mother was always afraid the tailors could see into their outdoor toilet. Half of the tiny backyard was bricked. An open gutter carried kitchen wastewater to a ditch in the middle of the yard, where it soaked into the waste from the outdoor toilet. The pump used to draw the family's water was not far from the wastewater site.

Bertie was the youngest child and had to entertain himself. He escaped into the gloomy backyard, spending hours creating battles on dirt piles that he imagined were ash-covered mountains. He fashioned armed soldiers from eggshells, tins, and boxes salvaged from the family trash.

Sometimes Bertie's wars were not imaginary. The youngest of three boys, he had to defend his possessions and play areas. When his brothers used his toys, Bertie struck back by biting and scratching them or kicking their legs. One time he threw a fork that stuck in his older brother Frank's forehead and left marks. In another rage, Bertie threw a wooden horse at his brother Freddy and broke a window. The older brothers sometimes placed pillows over Bertie's head until he grew short of breath.

Sarah Wells was not happy when Bertie was born. She did not want more children. But Bertie was an obviously precocious child and she took a great interest in his education.

Sarah Wells wanted her youngest son to learn a trade.

Maybe this intelligent son would redeem her life from the misery and despair she often felt because of the poverty—and because of her husband's inability to improve his family's circumstances. She taught three-year-old Bertie to read and write. His first written word was *butter*. He also liked to draw.

Despite the poor education he received, reading was one of Bertie's favorite occupations. When he was seven an accident provided him more time to read. At a cricket match one of his father's friends picked the youngster up, threw him into the air, and caught him. When the man tried it a second time, Bertie fell and landed on a tent peg, breaking his leg. In order for the bone to knit properly he had to lie inactive for several weeks. His father got books from the library to keep Bertie occupied. He particularly enjoyed looking through an astronomy book and studying pictures in a natural history book.

People knew Joseph Wells, Bertie's father, as a strong-willed man who made such an impression that others barely noticed his wife, who was quiet and serious. Their relationship was very much in tune with Victorian times. During this era men were considered the heads of households and women were expected to be submissive.

The crockery business was not profitable. Joseph, an avid cricket fan and player, began to stock sporting supplies. He also earned extra money as a professional cricket bowler and instructor. Gradually, bats and balls replaced jampots and tea sets in the shop's display window. But nothing Joseph did seemed to change the family's financial situation for long.

Joseph Wells attempted to support his family as a cricket bowler.

In his autobiography, H. G. described his mother as "a little blue-eyed, pink-cheeked woman with a large serious innocent face," who was fascinated with Queen Victoria. She went on and on about Her Highness's clothes, housing, and other possessions. Often she would take her three sons into the street so they could watch the queen pass in her carriage. This hero worship angered Bertie. He could not understand why the royal family should have so much when his family had so little.

By age ten Bertie was showing an interest in writing. He created an illustrated children's story he called "The Desert Daisy." It was about a war whose participants were the royal family, Anglican Church officials, and military officers. He also wrote some historical essays and parodies of magazines. His talent made him a pet of Mr. Morley, which alienated him from the other schoolboys.

Another accident added to the family's troubles. In 1877 Bertie's father was attempting to prune a grapevine in the backyard. To reach the highest shoots, he balanced a ladder on a bench. He lost his footing and fell to the ground. Two neighbors helped carry him upstairs. The doctor identified the break as a compound fracture of the thigh. The crippling injury ended what income Joseph had been earning from playing cricket. With this new hardship, the family often sat down to a supper of bread and cheese, or a breakfast of half a herring each with bread and butter, or a midday hash made up mainly of potatoes.

The life around him began to diminish Bertie's faith in

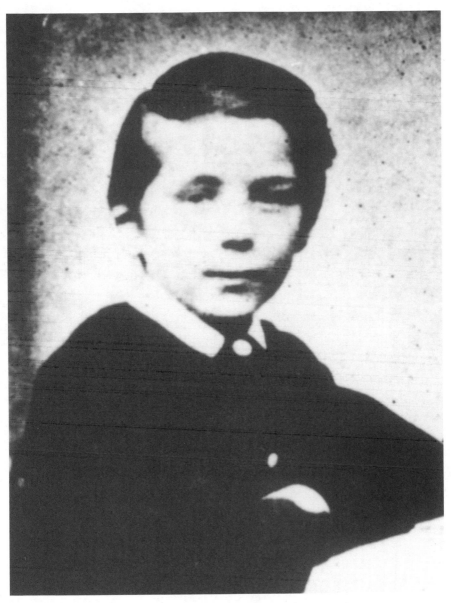

At age ten Bertie wrote his first story, "The Desert Daisy."

religion. In a magazine he learned of a man being tortured on something called the wheel. It slowly turned, dipping the man into fire. That night in bed, he dreamt a nightmare in which the culprit performing the torture was God. It dawned on him that God had to be in charge of the bad things that befell people as well as the good. Such a being did not make sense. Bertie could no longer agree with organized religion. He began to believe in a world without God.

After Joseph's accident Sarah returned to domestic service. She had been a maid before her marriage, and in 1880 the woman she had previously worked for hired her as a live-in housekeeper. Now, probably with a sense of relief, Sarah moved to the estate called Up Park and began to earn living expenses. Meanwhile, Joseph remained at home, helpless both as a wage earner and as a cricket player.

Sarah did not want her son to be like his father. She thought he needed a skill that would provide him work. He was a bright boy, but she was afraid that if he continued in school he would be too old to learn a job. So when Bertie was thirteen she arranged for him to become an apprentice. This meant that he would work in a shop for no pay. In return he would learn a trade. His two older brothers had also been apprenticed.

Bertie went to work as a draper's assistant in Windsor, near Windsor Castle. He was the cashier in the front room, a job that included dusting and window cleaning. Bertie helped prepare the day's cash sheet. At the end of the day, he helped balance the sheet and swept the shop floor. The boys were free until 10:00 with lights out at 10:30. The shop was closed Sundays.

Because Bertie did not enjoy the work, he often day-dreamed. He made errors on the cash sheets. In a letter to his mother he complained:

> We sleep 4 together, 3 apprentices & 1 of the hands in one room (of course no separate beds). We lay in bed until 7:30 when a bell rings & we jump up & put trousers slippers socks & jacket on over nightgown & hurry down & dust the shop. About 8:15 we hurry upstairs & dress & wash for breakfast. At 8:30 we go into a sort of vault underground (lit by gas) & have breakfast. After breakfast I am in the shop & desk till dinner at 1 (we have dinner underground as well as breakfast) & then work till tea (which we have in the same place) & then go on to supper at 8:30 at which time work is done & we may then go out until 10:30 at which time the apprentices are obliged to be in the house. I don't like the place much for it is not at all like home.

Bertie sneaked books to the work area. Sometimes he crept off to the warehouse where he could read undisturbed, or hid among the tall stacks of cloth. This behavior did not go unnoticed. Eventually the drapers refused to work with him any longer and he was sent home.

While Bertie's mother was deciding what to do with her son next, a family friend called Uncle Williams had a suggestion. Williams was about to head up a school in the town of Somerset that would prepare young boys for the national exams. In those days, teachers employed pupil teachers to help with the work. After four years of this, the pupil teachers could enter a teacher training college. He offered to let Bertie became a pupil teacher.

Uncle Williams was a colorful character. Great tufts of hair grew out of his ears. He had only one arm. The stump had a hook screwed in the end that could be removed and replaced with a special fork when it was time to eat.

At the Wookey School, some of the students were as big as fourteen-year-old Bertie. They made fun of his Kentish accent. Bertie sometimes hit students to keep them in line. One time he chased a misbehaving student all the way to the child's home.

The missing arm was not Uncle Williams's only unusual trait. Sometimes he entered class and yelled a weather report, then left for an extended time. Area residents saw him talking to himself in public. In addition, his educational background was very limited. Not surprisingly, the school closed in less than a year.

Back at Up Park, Bertie was free to wander along the halls and tunnels of the great home. The servants liked and humored him. He had plenty of time for reading. He read Swift's *Gulliver's Travels*, Thomas Paine's *Common Sense* and *The Rights of Man*, and Plato's *Republic*. He even created a household newspaper called the *Up Park Alarmist*. It made fun of life at the mansion. Some of the servants laughed at his humor; others thought he should be punished.

After two years there, Bertie tried another apprenticeship,

this time with a druggist. The firm was located three hours away from Up Park. Because the prescriptions would be written in Latin, Bertie was sent to Midhurst School, run by Mr. Horace Byatt, to learn Latin. Byatt soon realized that Bertie was an exceptional student.

When he was finished with the Latin training, Bertie worked at the druggist's for a short time until he was dismissed.

Sarah found another placement in the drapery business, this time with Southsea Drapery Emporium. Bertie was determined not to complete the apprenticeship. He did not want to be doomed to the dismal life of a draper. Bertie's job was to straighten cloth stock, pack it up after showings, and return it to storage. His performance was sloppy. Early morning chores were similar to those at the previous drapery shop. Sometimes he was sent to other shops for supplies, a welcome relief from everyday toil. Bertie's supervisors could often be heard asking, "What is Wells doing? Where on earth is that boy now?"

Bertie worked at the Southsea Drapery Emporium for two years. He hated every moment, especially the domineering tyranny of his superiors. He was also bothered by the class-consciousness of clerks. They wore the formal attire of general merchants but, in reality, were not accepted at that social level. The strict class system of Victorian England always reminded people of their true standing in society.

As he entered his second year, Bertie wanted to "Get out of this trade [drapery] before it is too late. At any cost get out of it." He wrote to Horace Byatt, the headmaster who had taught him Latin at Midhurst, and asked, "Might I not be useful in the school?" Byatt offered him the position of student assistant in the grammar school.

Bertie walked the many miles home that very weekend and begged his mother to release him from his apprenticeship. She was afraid that his leaving the apprenticeship would reflect poorly on the family's reputation but she finally agreed. Bertie had escaped a life in the drapery business. On his train ride to Midhurst, seventeen-year-old Herbert George Wells wrote a song about the Southsea Drapery Emporium and his employer, John Key, that matched the train's rhythm. He later recalled that it went something like this:

Puff and rumble old J.K. Old J.K. Old J.K.
Damn-the-boy has got away, *got* away, *got* away
Damn-the-boy has got away, got away forever.

Chapter Two

From Pupil to Teacher

At seventeen Bertie, who would soon be known as the more mature sounding H. G., was "...a slight, fair youth, with untidy hair and clothes, and a downy chin and upper lip....As an individual he was...reserved but friendly, quickly attracting people to him...."

The early Midhurst days were glorious. H. G. was productive. He even created lists of tasks for each hour of the day. Byatt taught in the same room as H. G. and gave him many helpful hints about teaching. H. G. described Byatt as "an energetic capable teacher, a large full-faced man, with a deeply cleft chin, impressive domed forehead beneath a receding hair, bright alert eyes, and in the firm lips a hint of both irascibility and humour."

In the evenings, H. G. attended Byatt's classes. The schoolmaster's style was to put good textbooks in the hands of students and have them read while he worked at his desk. H. G. studied human physiology, vegetable physiology, geology, inorganic chemistry, and math. As H. G. studied the courses, he discovered that he liked science.

The young pupil-teacher re-read Plato's *Republic*, which offered a reasoned argument to support H. G.'s doubts about religion as well as guided him toward questioning the way current society was organized. This was a time of severe labor unrest, with many job layoffs and strikes. In England the two largest social classes were still the upper and the lower. Most of the people in the lower class were attempting to struggle into the growing middle but it was difficult. Hundreds of years of tradition weighted them down. His reading encouraged H. G. to think about such important questions as "By *what right*—is this for you and not for me?" He also read Henry George's *Progress and Poverty*, that argued the community, not individuals, should profit from land and capital. Bertie Wells was becoming a socialist.

Joseph Wells showed genuine interest in H. G.'s academic successes and in the philosophical and scientific ideas his son wanted to discuss. Although he limped and needed a cane, Joseph was now able to get around. On Sundays they packed a cold lunch and went for long walks. As a schoolboy, H. G. had sensed Joseph as far above him, as someone with whom he did not have a strong connection. But as a student at Midhurst, he saw his father differently. "He was bald and blue-eyed, with a rosy and cheerful face and a square beard like King David," H. G. recalled later.

Joseph Wells had learned to get along on his own without his wife. He read widely, enjoying the *Daily News* and *Longman's Magazine*, two popular periodicals of the time, and checked out books from the local library. He kept his mind active by playing chess, studying algebra, and learning botany and natural history. H. G. was often amazed at Joseph's broad knowledge of nature as they walked in the countryside.

H. G. submitted an application for a scholarship at the Normal School of Science in South Kensington. He received an acceptance notice. He would be studying under the famous science teacher T. H. Huxley. H. G. was awed to be in his new teacher's presence: "When I saw him so close, so familiarly present to me, I became excessively agitated with pride, and mighty respect for him."

As the eighteen-year-old entered London in 1884, he "was callow and cautious.... a little underweight—and had a scrawny, even cadaverous appearance. His skin was pale....[he] blushed very easily, and when he did he would often rub the back of his hand across his face to try to disguise his embarrassment."

The first time H. G. saw the biological laboratory at the Normal School he realized that until this point all the science he had learned had been secondhand. Now he would be learning firsthand, the way scientists learn. That year H. G. scored among the highest in his class on exams. For the first time he was meeting others as interested in science as he was.

During his stay at the Normal School, H. G. lost weight. Five feet and five inches tall, he weighed less than eight stone (112 pounds.) Normal meals were a poached egg and toast in the morning and a meat-tea at five in the evening, with bread and cheese in-between. Not realizing that his thin appearance was a product of malnutrition, H. G. assumed that he had a naturally inferior body. His true problem was poverty. The

Normal School paid training teachers twenty shillings a week. After expenses, H. G. was lucky to have a shilling for all the midday meals. If his money ran out a day or two before payday, Wells would simply fast until he got paid. His friend Jennings noted this and insisted on treating H. G. to a large restaurant meal. H. G. accepted gratefully the first time, but after that he refused because he did not want to be indebted.

The young scholar visited his Aunt Mary and her sister. He enjoyed tea with his aunt and a girl his age. In his autobiography he recalled that "...she had a grave and lovely face, very firmly modelled, broad brows and a particularly beautiful mouth and chin and neck." She was his cousin Isabel Wells.

Aunt Mary offered to let H. G. stay in an upstairs room. This lodging arrangement continued for the rest of H. G.'s school career. When he had time, he walked to classes accompanied by Isabel as she went to her job at a photograph-retouching studio. Gradually the two became romantically involved. In England during the 1880s, it was not as much a taboo for cousins to date as it might be today.

At school H. G. enjoyed Huxley's classes. He thought each class was a challenge. There were some classes, however, that did not meet his expectations. When he entered Professor Guthrie's physics class he was disappointed. Guthrie was slow moving and often seemed to be in a daze. The professor did not have a questioning mind. His lectures always came directly from textbooks but were still so inadequate they had to be supplemented by the assistant professor, who talked so rapidly that he could barely be understood. Professor Guthrie assumed students should construct their own lab materials.

H. G. attended the Normal School for Science in South Kensinton.

Handed a blowpipe, some glass tubing, a slab of wood, and some paper and brass pieces, H. G. had to make a barometer. The only thing H. G. learned from all this was that heated glass stays hot after it loses its redness. At the end of the course, in spite of high grades, H. G. felt he had learned almost nothing about physics.

Geology under Professor Judd went no better than physics. H. G. complained in his autobiography that "Judd was a better teacher than Guthrie, but he was a slow, conscientious lecturer with a large white face, small pale blue eyes, a habit of washing his hands with invisible water as he talked, and a flat voice. His eye watched you and seemed to take no interest in what his deliberate voice was saying."

The geology course required H. G. to memorize long lists and identifications. He did not like this less exciting work. Professor Judd made no effort to connect the long lists to the concepts and theories that would make the material come alive. Some parts of the class were worthwhile, however. When H. G. studied rock samples under a microscope, he said, "[Microscopes] let me into the very heart of those specimen chunks of rock one found so boring in a drawer, they lit them up with a blaze of glorious colour.... It was not simply an astounding loveliness, it was...a profoundly significant loveliness...." But there was rarely enough time for such appreciation.

Despite his interest in Huxley's classes, H. G. saw no overall purpose in the maze of labs and classrooms he took at the Normal School. As a result, after the first year his grades

Studying science with the famous Professor T. H. Huxley was the high-point of Bertie's education.

began to slide. The unchallenging courses were changing him from a learner thirsting after scientific knowledge to an indifferent pupil.

H. G. became a rebel. During lectures he created noises with rubber blowpipe tubes. These performances often drew applause from classmates. He began hanging around with witty friends from the Debating Society. At one point, after H. G. angered fellow debaters with offensive remarks, he was carried struggling from the room. But with the exception of his hair being pulled by someone, H. G. enjoyed the expulsion.

He and his friends began wearing red ties, which indicated that they believed in socialism, a system of government in which the land and businesses are controlled by the state rather than by private enterprise. They went to meetings of the Fabian Society, a group that had been organized in England to promote socialist ideas.

H. G.'s exam scores were poor at the end of his second year, and there was some question whether he would be allowed to return to the Normal School. But he was given another chance. During vacation break, H. G. worked on plans to present a Debating Society paper on socialism. He wanted to encourage his friends to believe as he did.

In his third year H. G. spent little time studying. Instead, he spent a great deal of time on political ideas. H. G. and his friends started the *Science Schools Journal*. He was its first editor. The first issue sold out but students ignored future issues, which disappointed H. G. Then he tried to focus on

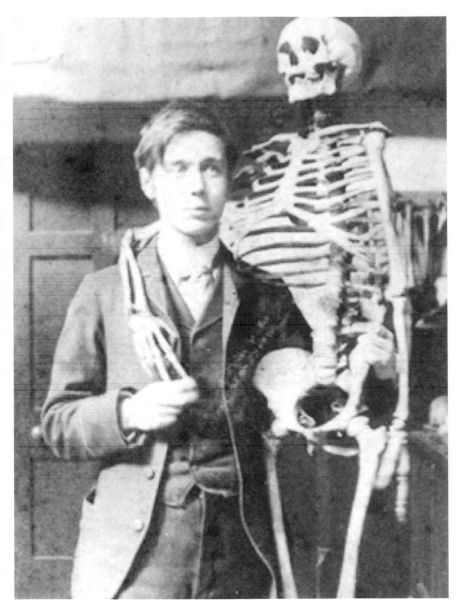

H. G. was expelled from the Normal School when he was twenty-one because of low grades and a propensity for practical jokes.

rock samples, but the socialist ideas interested him more.

In June 1887, his third year at the Normal School, H. G. was expelled because of low grades. He was twenty-one. He had done everything possible to earn this dismissal. Yet when it came, he was surprised. He felt lost. "What is to become of me *now*?" he wondered.

H. G. continued to write. Most of his work imitated other not very good writing he had read. He did manage to get one short story published. He remembered it only as a second-rate piece that appeared in the *Family Herald*, a well-known fiction magazine.

Meanwhile, he had to make a living. In the 1880s it was possible to teach school without a university degree. The Holt Academy in Wales needed a teacher. It included both a boys' and girls' secondary school, but its main purpose was to train young men for the ministry. They offered him a job and he accepted. It seemed an ideal way to heal the wounds of recent failure.

H. G. soon realized that he was not going to be any happier at the Holt Academy than he had been at the Normal School. The school was losing ground. The surroundings were ugly. The building's broken windows remained unmended. The headmaster was slovenly and often arrived at work drunk. H. G. had to share a bedroom with two ministry candidates. His students were crowded two or three to a bed. The meals were horrible. Still, he did his best to adapt: "I improvised lessons in the boys' school and in the girls' school, I taught scripture on Sunday afternoons, played cricket and Association football [rugby] to the best of my ability, and made my first attendances at a Calvinistic Methodist service [a job requirement]." But as he had as a draper's apprentice, H. G. felt trapped.

One of his students at Holt was A. A. Milne, who later wrote the Winnie the Pooh stories. Milne considered Wells a poor teacher because he lacked patience with the slower students.

Writing became more of an obsession. H. G. labored over some short stories and a novel he called *Lady Frankland's Companion*. He also met a girl named Annie Meredith—"a pretty girl, minister's daughter, teacher in a high school." While Isabel waited in London, H. G. carried on a relationship with Annie until she broke up with him over differing views on religion and politics.

Again an unfortunate accident worked in H. G.'s favor. One day while playing football one of the youths shouldered him and sent him flying and there was intense pain on one side of his abdomen. Later he found considerable blood in his urine and developed a raging fever. A doctor diagnosed that the left kidney had been crushed. Recovery meant a long stay in bed.

The immediate problem was finding a place to recuperate. His father was selling his house in Bromley. Because of a hearing loss, his mother would soon be leaving her job at Up Park. With no place to go, H. G. decided to continue teaching. But he developed a severe cough, which forced up blood. Even though the doctor said he had tuberculosis, H. G. was determined to finish out the term.

Eventually, the employers of H. G.'s mother agreed that he could recover at Up Park. He left his teaching position and spent four months in a room next to his mother. The doctor at Up Park did not agree with the tuberculosis diagnosis. He was more concerned with the crushed kidney and the possibility of diabetes.

Joseph Wells moved from Bromley to a small cottage three miles from Up Park. H. G.'s older brother Frank had quit the draper trade and was living with Joseph. When the middle brother Freddie came home for Christmas holidays, the entire family enjoyed their time together. They attended the Christmas dinner at Up Park. There, in spite of his illness, H. G. did some dancing.

The invalid spent four months reading poetry and other literature. This reading gave him a chance to view his own writing more objectively, and to experiment. He recalled the experience in his autobiography: "I began to observe and imitate. I read everything accessible. I ground out some sonnets. I struggled with Spenser; I read Shelley, Keats, Heine, Whitman, Lamb, Holmes, Stevenson, Hawthorne, and a number of popular novels. I began to realize the cheapness and flatness of my own phrasing." Eventually, he burned his earlier writings.

He continued writing letters to friends that revealed discouragement about his writing and his career. In one letter he listed all items he had written to date, along with a record of what happened to each. All but one piece had been burned, lost, or sent out with no return. The single short story he sold

H. G. recuperated from an illness at Up Park, the estate where his mother was employed.

to the *Family Herald* had earned him one pound. He added, "Some day I shall succeed, but it is a weary game." In another letter he lashed out at a now familiar target: "I have a faint idea that God has sent all this to chasten me. If so he has certainly mistaken his man. I have learnt some wholesome lessons in human charity, but I repudiate God more than ever. He's a beggar, he is."

After four months at Up Park H. G. stayed another three months with married friends in their guestroom. When he protested that he was too much of a bother, both the husband and the wife pointed out that his entertaining monologues about life in school and at Up Park were more than payment enough. While staying with the friends, H. G. changed his attitude. "I have been dying for nearly two-thirds of a year," he reflected, "and I have died enough." He borrowed money from his mother and in 1888 set off to secure a job in London.

In London his first task was to get a room. He rented part of an attic that contained a pullout bed, washstand, chair, and chest of drawers with looking glass. Sounds traveled easily between the walls dividing his quarters from the others.

He signed up with employment agencies and began to answer ads. The only jobs that came through were some tutoring assignments. An old Normal School friend named Jennings was working as a science coach. He hired H. G. to draw some wall diagrams to be used as teaching equipment.

Once he had some money, H. G. wrote Isabel and asked if he could visit. By now her family had moved into new quarters. There was a room H. G. could use, so he left his attic room and moved into his aunt's home, where he and Isabel resumed their romance.

Because of his precarious health, he felt he could not rely on teaching for a regular income. H. G. was determined to make his living as a writer. Penny weekly magazines were popular at the time. One of them contained a column called "Questions Worth Answering" that encouraged the readers to send in questions that the column could answer. Published questions or answers earned a small payment—the longer the answer, the more the payment. A truly ambitious writer might be able to write his own question and then answer it. Using this method, H. G. earned anywhere from two to fifteen shillings a week.

When another teaching opportunity arose in 1889, H. G. needed money so badly that he could not pass it up. Henley House in London was a private boys' school that catered to children of businessmen, professionals, and people in the arts. Most of the students commuted from home instead of living on the grounds. H. G. was hired to teach science.

To his disappointment H. G. became so busy with teaching that he had little time to write. He left Henley House to join the University Correspondence College of Cambridge. The Correspondence College arranged for teachers to coach university-examination candidates through the mail. The pay increase allowed him to set a wedding date with Isabel. The couple married on October 31, 1891.

Chapter Three

Journalism

Soon the marriage was in trouble. H. G. was impulsive, while Isabel tended to move slowly and cautiously through life. She did not understand why he complained so much about his job at the correspondence school. She wanted to settle into a typical married life. She also could not understand why he spent hours slaving away at his own writing. Why would H. G. want to write more things when he already had so much correspondence work to do? Their different attitudes toward life and the future caused tension. Conversation between them gradually lessened. They no longer talked anything but small, risk-free domestic subjects.

As his interest in Isabel dwindled, H.G. met Amy Catherine Robbins, a tutorial student. He later remembered her as "a fragile figure, with very delicate features, very fair hair and very brown eyes." Amy was different than Isabel. She was one of a new generation of young women who planned to establish an independent career. She agreed with H. G.'s ideas about socialism and how best to assure human progress. They had challenging discussions that led to meetings after class. Discussing their ideas and exchanging books and notes, the two developed emotional attachments. H. G. realized that he wanted a life with Amy Robbins, not with Isabel.

Amy Catherine Robbins was the only daughter of a conventional family who found the demands of Victorian society exasperating. Working for her college degree in science was part of her revolt against the accepted ideas about women and their roles in society. It was these scientific and philosophical ideas that fired the developing romance between teacher and student, not sexual attraction. They were partners in an intellectual adventure. They had something else in common—neither was in the best of health. They felt desperate to spend as much time together as possible.

One night in 1890, going home late after a tutorial class, H. G. began coughing up blood. The fit continued throughout the night. Then he went into a deep sleep. When he awoke much later he felt strangely peaceful. The experience led him to decide there could be no more teaching or tutoring. Now he would have to make a living by writing. "No more teaching for me forever," he wrote his friend Elizabeth Healey.

He agonized over his decision to leave teaching for writing, and with good reason. His father had been an excellent cricket player but a poor provider. Often the household had teetered on the brink of financial ruin. When Joseph finally lost the business, H. G.'s mother had been forced to resume work as a domestic servant. The financial difficulties had been a huge strain. Had the father's flaw—his inability to maintain a steady career—become the son's? Apprenticed three times,

H. G. had failed in each. He had been asked to leave the Normal School of Science because of poor grades. At this crucial time in his life, he felt desperate for success.

His family was also suffering new difficulties. His mother had been dismissed from her position at Up Park. His father had been living for several years in a cottage near Up Park with no hope of employment. His brother Frank was living with him and barely making ends meet in his small clock-repairing business, and Freddy had recently been let go by his drapery establishment because the owner's son would be taking over the business. One-third of H. G.'s income was being used to help the family.

Earlier the editor Frank Harris had published a paper H. G. had written during his college debating days called "The Rediscovery of the Unique." H. G. decided to send him a follow-up essay called "Universe Rigid." After receiving the manuscript Harris summoned H. G. to his office.

Nervous about the appointment, H. G. decided he should dress up for the occasion. He carried an umbrella and wore a morning coat. His hat looked scruffy and old from misuse. He hurriedly brushed it and wiped it down with a silk handkerchief. Still not satisfied, he used a sponge on it and went out into the world sporting a wet hat.

After an hour's wait, he was ushered into a large room. Harris's black hair was "parted in the middle and brushed fiercely back. He had a blunt nose over a vast black upturned moustache, from beneath which came a deep voice of exceptional power."

Soon after his marriage to Isabel, H. G. knew that he had made a mistake.

When he entered the office Harris bellowed, "And it was *you* sent me this Universe R-R-Rigid!" As H. G. set his hat upon the table he realized what a sorry sight it was. The shine had disappeared. Drying had occurred only in spots, leaving dark wet patches. Harris looked at it, then forced his eyes back to Wells. "You sent me this Universe Gur-R-R-Rigid," he repeated. "Dear Gahd! I can't understand six words of it. What do you *mean* by it? For Gahd's sake tell me what it is all *about*?" He knocked on the manuscript with his hand.

"Well, you see—" Wells began to explain.

"I don't see. That's just what I don't see."

H. G. tried again: "The idea—if you consider time is space, then—I mean if you treat it like a fourth dimension like, well then you see...."

At the end of the discussion, Harris rejected the manuscript.

When he got back home H. G. tore the hat to pieces. Maybe it had brought him bad luck.

His brother Fred moved to South Africa and established himself as a business agent. He promised to send money that would help support the parents. This eased the pressure on H. G., however, his health was still bad, and the tension created by the developing relationship with Amy Robbins was growing. He decided to splurge on a much needed vacation to the seaside.

It was at the beach that he made the breakthrough which would make his journalism career successful. Reading J. M. Barrie's *When a Man's Single,* he found a section of the book where one of the characters discussed how his ideas for writing came from everyday events, not lofty ideas. It dawned on H. G. that "for years I had been seeking rare and precious topics.... The more I was rejected the higher my shots had flown. All the time I had been shooting over the target. All I had to do was lower my aim—and hit."

He quickly wrote a piece about vacationing at the seashore and the *Pall Mall Gazette* accepted it by return mail. The formula worked. Before long, H. G. was making more money through articles and reviews than he had been getting as a teacher. Editors wrote to H. G. asking for his articles.

In 1891, the editor of the *Pall Mall Gazette* asked to see H. G. As he approached the editor's office, he heard sobbing. The crier got up suddenly to greet H. G. Mr. Cust regained his composure and explained that he liked Wells's writing and wanted him to do some reviewing as soon as possible. Apparently he had forgotten all about the crisis that had caused his sobbing.

Cust introduced H. G. to Lewis Hind, editor of the *Pall Mall Budget*, an offshoot of the *Gazette*. Hind wanted H. G. to consider writing a series of weekly science articles. Cust suggested that H. G. go see another editor, W. E. Henley. Mr. Henley had a large body and small legs. He was extravagant and "he emphasized his remarks by clutching an agate paper weight in his big freckled paw and banging it on his writing table." Henley wanted H. G. to write for the *National Observer*. H. G. had in mind revising and submitting a story about time travel from his days as *Science Schools Journal* editor.

In December 1892, H. G. and Isabel visited Amy Robbins for three days. At the end of that visit, it was clear to Isabel that her husband and Amy were more than just friends. She demanded an end to the relationship, which he refused. This effectively ended the marriage. By January 1893 he was living with Amy Robbins. Both Isabel and H. G. regretted the rapid separation; but once they were on that course, there was no going back.

To escape the chaos surrounding his personal life, the newly successful journalist decided to draw on his savings and move out of London for the summer. Both he and Amy would benefit from sea air. No sooner had he left the city than he got a lesson in how quickly his fortunes could change. The *National Observer* hired a new editor who did not like H. G.'s writing and stopped using his articles. About the same time, the *Pall Mall Gazette* employed a temporary editor who also did not want Wells's work. Now H. G.'s monthly income was less than his monthly spending. The final blow came when the new *Pall Mall Budget* folded. As if this were not bad luck enough, the landlady at the seaside rooming house began to give H. G. and Amy a difficult time. She did not like them living under the same roof. Fortunately, they were able return to the apartment they had in London.

Chapter Four

Famous Novelist

W. E. Henley of the *National Observer* was going to start a monthly magazine. He told H. G. to rewrite his *Time Traveler* as a serial story. This meant that an episode would appear each week. It was a great deal of work to be done on a short deadline. H. G. set about redoing the book. Henley agreed to pay 100 pounds for serial rights. He also planned to recommend its full-length publication to a book-publishing company. Meanwhile, the *Pall Mall Gazette* began publishing H. G.'s work again. And editor Frank Harris, who had rejected "Universe Rigid," purchased the magazine *Saturday Review*. He contacted H. G. to write for him.

By August 1894, H. G. had stopped his work with the University Correspondence College. He also stopped writing about teaching for the *Journal of Education*. He was free to pursue free-lance writing full-time. He wanted to write more short stories, which paid better and produced more income when they were re-published in anthologies.

After leaving his post at the college, H. G. developed a consistent writing routine. He wrote daily, usually in the morning, always with pen or pencil on standard writing paper. Amy typed a copy of what he'd written at midday. In the afternoon H. G. would edit the typescript, adding or taking out phrases and words. His most common change was to add further explanation. Once the revised copy had been typed, the piece was ready for the printer.

H. G.'s divorce from Isabel became final and he married Amy Catherine, whom by now he had nicknamed "Jane." The couple soon worked out compromises in their relationship. Jane was his typist and first copy editor. She also took charge of all money matters. She eventually came to understand that he wanted his sexual freedom, but that in the end he would always return to her. H. G. later described this arrangement in his autobiography, "All life is imperfect: imperfection becomes a condemnation only when it reaches an intolerable level. Our imperfections we made quite tolerable and I do not believe that in making them tolerable we injured anybody else in the world." H. G. and Jane remained married until her death.

In years to come, H. G. would explore his theory of sexuality through writing. For example, his novel *Love and Mr. Lewisham* (1900) traces a character's feelings of being trapped in married life. In *Sea Lady* (1902), love leads to a breaking-up instead of a settling-down, and defeat is the result. One of the consistent themes in H. G.'s novels was his attempt to develop a philosophy of successful love and mar-riage—or of male-female relationships in general.

The couple's early married days were frugal but happy. Their first apartment had a single bedroom opening onto a

H. G. and Amy Catherine Robbins were married in 1894.

living room. H. G. worked at a small table in a corner of the bedroom or at a larger table in the living room. They had no private bathroom; instead, they bathed in a washtub. They invented nicknames for each other and often talked in a created dialect somewhat akin to baby talk. H. G. was forever inventing humorous pieces that in this dialect he called "pomes" and making drawings that he called "picshuas."

H. G. had trouble maintaining a consistent routine. His schedule tended to be irregular, a few productive days followed by a few less productive ones. On good days H. G. spent the morning writing his reviews or articles. Once he was finished with a draft Jane typed it. If there was no typing, she went shopping for groceries or wrote or studied for her college courses. In this way he was able to complete about three articles a week. Around noon the couple went walking in a park or among the many shops in the area. They would go out in search of topics for H. G.'s articles. They looked in unusual places, such as cemeteries or museums or wooded areas. They went to art shows and the zoo. Later in the day they played board or card games. They could not afford to go to concerts and plays.

But financial success was on the horizon. H. G.'s revised time travel story, now titled *The Time Machine,* was serialized in 1895. It was an immediate success that changed twenty-nine-year-old H. G.'s prospects as a writer overnight. One reviewer called him "a man of genius." Another claimed that at last someone had written "a new thing under the sun." As this first novel hit the stores, he was working on another scientific romance he called *The Island of Doctor Moreau.* He got the idea for this story from a magazine article he had written about surgery. He was also making notes on one called *The Wonderful Visit*, which was suggested to him when another author remarked that an angel visiting earth would be shot.

H. G.'s interest in science and how it would affect the future was a theme that connected with readers approaching the end of the nineteenth century. In both his fiction and nonfiction Wells was able to raise ethical and moral questions about science and its impact on human existence in works with themes postulated from his scientific research. This combination of scientific and technological speculation with moral questioning is the centerpiece of a genre now called science fiction. Many consider H. G. to be the father of science fiction because, unlike Jules Verne who wrote earlier, he tried to adhere to plots that were at least scientifically plausible.

Although he was in many ways ahead of his time, H. G.'s career was made possible because of the technological changes that were rapidly altering the world around him. The benefits of the industrial revolution were finally reaching the mass of people in Europe and America. Machines shortened the workweek while electricity lengthened the day. Fewer work hours meant more leisure time, which some people used to acquire knowledge and to work on self-improvement. More people were attending schools for longer periods of time. This raised literacy rates. The more educated were hungry for new ideas to be presented in ways they could understand. H. G., with his fascination for ideas and his skill at storytelling and communicating scientific information in easily understood language, was a perfect writer for the thousands of new readers. This change in society also coincided with production of cheap paper that made it a perfect time for publishing.

H. G.'s novels reflected a scientific understanding and questioning that echoed concerns addressed in his nonfiction. Two essays, for example, "A Vision of the Past" and "The Extinction of Man," dealt with issues raised in his fiction. He was becoming convinced that scientists got at the truth better than politicians. Socialism appealed to H. G. and Jane because of its scientific approach to helping the poor have a better life. They became convinced that it would take a socialist revolution to set matters right.

In 1895 the Wellses moved into a new home in Woking, near a railroad line. There H. G. completed *War of the Worlds*, *Wheels of Chance,* and *The Invisible Man,* which was based on a poem by W.S. Gilbert called "The Perils of Invisibility."

After a year and a half in Woking, the couple needed a larger home. Jane's ill mother had to move in with them. Their new house at Worcester Park contained two large rooms on the first floor, a guestroom, and a good-sized garden. Now they could entertain friends regularly on weekends. Jane kept the house in order and kept bothersome visitors away so H. G. could work.

In September 1897, when H. G. was thirty-one, he received a letter from a writer named Arnold Bennett. This was the beginning of an enduring friendship. The two writers were about the same age, were dedicated to their craft of writing,

H. G. concentrated on the relationship between science and morality in the new genre, "science fiction."

and had grown up in lower-middle-class backgrounds. Both thought that good writing resulted from applying straightforward, uncomplicated craft and writing style to interesting themes.

In 1898 H. G. and Jane took a bicycle trip to southern England. During the trip, H. G. caught a cold. His injured kidney acted up and he developed a temperature. The doctor prescribed surgery, but the surgeon could find no reason to operate. The kidney problem had seemed to take care of itself. During his convalescence, H. G. wrote a children's book entitled *The Story of Tommy and the Elephant* for his doctor's infant daughters. It was published years later.

H. G. had established a pattern of feverish work followed by relapses due to ill health, followed again by feverish work. He developed the habit of pushing toward deadlines during his days in journalism. He took great satisfaction from making money. It was rewarding to keep Jane and his family comfortable, and to pay for the material possessions he enjoyed, such as homes, books, and clothes.

H. G. and Jane became active in the Fabian Society, the group of socialists that H. G. had learned of while at the Normal School. They made friends with Sidney and Beatrice Webb, the founders of the group. They also met the future great playwright, George Bernard Shaw, who was a confidant of the Webbs. H. G. and Shaw were friendly with each other, but there was always a distance between them. They had similar lower-middle-class backgrounds and thought that society needed to be reorganized on a more equitable basis.

Sidney and Beatrice Webb founded the Fabian Society, a group that supported socialist principles.

But H. G. never was able to rid himself of a slight mistrust of Shaw. He also thought that Shaw's famous humor tended to reduce important topics to witty conversational tidbits. Wells was much more earnest in his beliefs than was Shaw.

H. G. felt himself pulled in two directions. On the one hand, he was attracted to the world of social science, which Sidney and Beatrice Webb wrote about. The Webbs and H. G. created another group—the Coefficients—that met to dine and debate about the British Empire. He was also tugged toward his more artistic side, which focused on the creation of new forms and ideas. He struggled between the two roles, maintaining friendships with fiction writers Stephen Crane, Ford Madox Ford, and Joseph Conrad while participating in the Fabians and the Coefficients.

H. G. read a great deal about socialism and gradually came to see it in a way that differed from the ideas of the Fabians. The Fabians were essentially an upper-class group of intellectuals. They thought that the best way to move society toward socialism was by influencing the way political and other leaders thought. The Webbs were proud of the influence they had over powerful government officials. They thought an elite group such as theirs would benefit those who did not have access to powerful politicians in Great Britain.

H. G., on the other hand, came to think that the elitism of the Fabians was its greatest weakness. He thought that the leadership of the group should be expanded to include more people like him—lower-middle-class and working-class thinkers who had proven that they were entitled to a leadership role.

Although they had similar backgrounds, H. G. was always distrustful of George Bernard Shaw.

Wells believed in a merit-based society and thought the Webbs still clung to old notions of a class-based society.

When H. G. joined the Fabian Society, it was difficult to be granted membership. He had to be recommended by a member and then have two other members endorse his membership. Then he had to wait for a vote. It took a long time; clearly the system was set up to tightly control membership. He wanted to open this procedure. He also wanted to remove some of the leaders and replace them with members who agreed with his ideas. Before long it became clear that H. G. wanted to be in control of the Fabian Society.

A leadership battle ensued with Wells and a few supporters on one side and the Webbs on the other. For a period of time Shaw was a middleman, attempting to seek points of agreement between the two camps. Eventually, after many speeches had been delivered and many letters written, it became clear that Shaw was siding with the Webbs. Soon it also became clear that H. G. had no chance of garnering a majority of support from the members.

H. G. was his own worst opponent during the struggle with the Webbs. He refused to discuss compromise whenever Shaw would present a proposal. Many members agreed with H. G. that the society needed to be rearranged and opened up. Even the Webbs agreed initially and hoped that H. G. would help bring in more members like himself. But H. G. insisted on delivering insulting and defamatory speeches in his thin, high-pitched voice, even when Shaw and others pointed out that to do so would be counterproductive. His suggestions for reorganizing would have meant that the Webbs be ejected with no appreciation for the years of service they had given the society they created. In short, H. G. allowed his temper and argumentative personality to interfere with clear thinking. Beatrice Webb, who at one point said she would be relieved if someone took the responsibility of the group off of her and Sidney's shoulders, felt that H. G. could have won the Fabian power struggle if not for those two factors.

By the end of 1907 H. G. had withdrawn from active membership in the Fabian Society. He wanted socialism to be based on a belief system, not on the dictates of party politics. While he was involved in the group and helping to popularize it with his writing, membership increased fourfold; after he left, membership decreased.

H. G. did make close friends through his work with the Fabians. The closest was Graham Wallas, with whom he traveled to Switzerland on a vacation. Wallas loved to talk about ideas. But he had little self-discipline, so few of his written works were ever completed. The two men remained friends for more than thirty years.

Two other close friends H. G. made during this period were the couple Elizabeth and Hubert Bland. Hubert was a businessman from an old, noble family. Elizabeth was a writer with a brilliant mind that often made Hubert feel inadequate. To make up for his feeling of inferiority, Hubert Bland pursued other women.

Socialism was popular among young women in the 1880s because it advocated a stronger role for women in society.

Many of the young women who attended the Fabian lectures idolized H. G. Rosamund Bland, Elizabeth and Hubert's daughter, was among these admirers. She and Wells grew closer until they were having an affair. This relationship between the older Wells and the young student put a strain on the friendship between H. G. and the Blands. Eventually, Rosamund was married to another man.

Pember Reeves, another Fabian, had a young daughter named Amber who also pursued H. G. Initially he resisted her advances, but eventually they also became romantically involved. Amber's school studies deteriorated, and she dreamed of having a child by H. G. She soon became pregnant with H. G.'s child and married a young man of her own age who was aware of her pregnancy. Over the years she was an attentive mother to her three children, and later in life she and H. G. became good friends. Jane remained loyal to her husband throughout these public affairs.

H. G. and Jane decided to build the kind of house they wanted. It was designed so that the living rooms were on the same floor as the bedrooms. Given his health history, he realized he might someday be confined to a wheelchair and would find it difficult to mount stairs. After it was built, the new home was called Spade House because of a compromise made with the architect who was in the habit of identifying his homes by placing a heart on the door. H. G. did not want a heart, so a spade was placed on his door instead.

The couple moved into their new home on the Kent coast in 1900, when H. G. was thirty-four. It was within easy reach of London by train. After settling in H. G. began work on a new book—*Anticipations of the Reaction of Mechanical and Scientific Progress Upon Human Life and Thought* (*Anticipations* for short). He considered this one of his most important works. It was a natural follow-up to a theme found in some of his previous works, such as *Man of the Year Million* and *The Time Machine*. He called this theme the "Open Conspiracy." It was his effort to convince people to think and act in new ways.

The book starts with a look at how humans get along socially and how they carry out their business ventures. It then discusses how these elements influence others, such as politics, the world of work, and education. H. G. tried to make clear how the current social order was disintegrating without preparing another to take its place. He then traced the roots of democracy, which in its present state he saw as unworkable. Instead, he proposed "The New Republic." He also dealt with modern warfare in the book. A major emphasis was that "scientific and industrial progress" was way ahead of "political and social structures."

In *Anticipations*, H. G. was attempting to predict the direction human existence would take. Small-scale, specific predictions had been made in previous writings, but never one as grand as this. When it was published the book sold well and helped to seal his reputation as a social thinker as well as a novelist. "I was writing the human prospectus," he commented later. *Anticipations* was also an attempt to apply science to historical record making. H. G. had observed that the history of the time was simply a collection of facts mixed with rumor. True history—or "Human Ecology," as he called it—would pave our way into the future and give us an intelligent backdrop on which we could base decisions.

By 1900, H. G. was becoming more relaxed in his writing routine. His health had also improved. He enjoyed swimming, badminton, tennis, walking, cycling, and charades. Sometimes he worked all day for days in succession. Other times he played for extended periods. He experimented with different approaches to writing. He once tried to begin his writing session at 4:00 a.m., and another time he wrote while Jane played Beethoven piano sonatas. From 1901 to 1911, H. G. was a highly productive writer. He published *The First Men in the Moon* (1901), *Anticipations* (1901), *Mankind in the Making* (1903), *The Food of the Gods* (1904), *A Modern Utopia* (1905), *Kipps* (1905), *In the Days of the Comet* (1906), *The War in the Air* (1908), *Tono-Bungay* (1909), *Ann Veronica* (1909), *The History of Mr. Polly* (1910), and *The New Machiavelli* (1911).

H. G. and Jane's first son, G. P. Wells, or "Gip," as he was nicknamed, was born in 1901, six years after their wedding. Jane was in labor more than twenty-four hours. Frank, the second son, arrived in 1903. Early in their lives trained nurses tended to the boys. Later, as they developed into schoolboys, their mother became a steady companion and friend. This diminished the time she could spend with H. G.

The boys had plenty of room to play at Spade House. H. G. made up games and created toys to entertain his sons. In time,

From left to right, Frank (1903,) Jane, and Gip (1901,) Wells. Jane was a devoted mother to her sons.

the games were outlined in books. H. G. spent most weeks at an apartment he had rented in London, returning on the weekend for whatever festivities had been planned. He liked physical exercise on the weekends. The family went for long walks, sometimes to a museum, other times to visit friends. He read the boys bedtime stories, often illustrating them with his "picshuas." If there were visitors, they played games, some of them outdoors. On a typical weekend with visitors, the Wellses spent evenings playing charades or cards or performing original plays. There were also lengthy discussions or manuscript-reading sessions.

The Wellses began entertaining on weekends more frequently and Jane became an accomplished actress. She performed charades and impromptu roles at the parties they held at Spade House. "And through all this tangle of cheery burlesque," H. G. recalled, "goes my wife, gravely radiant and indefatigable. She had accumulated presses full of gaily coloured dressing up garments and her instinct for effect was unerring."

At one of their many weekend gatherings H. G. was given the charade "God moves in mysterious ways." He performed it by using a dinner table mat as a beard, then walking in an odd way. Observing this, a neighbor refused to let his children visit the Wells home in the future because its master had blasphemed God.

In January 1902, H. G. delivered a speech at the Royal Institution. Unfortunately, his poor speaking ability—a high, squeaky voice that delivered his speech too rapidly through a thick mustache—did not help his success. Even so, the audience was receptive. The speech was rushed into print and published as "Discovery of the Future." It sold 6,000 copies in the first month.

In this speech, Wells described two kinds of minds—forward-thinking and backward-thinking. He then tried to show that "the deliberate direction of historical study, and of economic and social study towards the future, and an increasing reference, a deliberate and courageous reference to the future in moral and religious discussion, would be enormously stimulating and enormously profitable to our intellectual life." His main message was that if we could collectively use all the knowledge at our disposal, we could manage the direction of change. It was a positive message. Writers like Joseph Conrad praised the speech. It established Wells as one of the most famous men of the new twentieth century.

A follow-up book to his highly successful *Anticipations* was *Mankind in the Making* (1903). This book moved from analyzing history to focusing on an overall view of human achievement. It recommended a new education system that would prepare for the "New Republic." H. G. admitted later that this book was more didactic than analytical.

Chapter Five

World War I

By 1912 the Wells family had moved from Spade House to Easton Glebe, a London neighborhood. H. G. sent his two sons to Oundle School. Frank began in 1912 and Gip in 1914, the first year of World War I.

Between 1895 and 1914 H. G. published thirty-two books, enough short stories to fill eight volumes, and dozens of newspaper and magazine articles. Jane helped make this productivity possible. She did his secretarial work, ran the household, and was the principal parent. In addition, she became a master gardener.

Between 1910 and 1913, H. G. had a relationship with the writer Grafin von Arnim, whom he referred to as "Little e." Irish by birth, the small and enthusiastic widow of a German count had sought out H. G. after reading one of his books. She left impressed after a sudden visit to his home while Jane was away. She said he was the most intelligent of her vast number of friends. Jane approved of Little e's books and had no qualms about the affair.

Little e had a chalet in Switzerland that H. G. visited often. There were always other guests when he visited, so she had a secret door installed in her bedroom. The two lovers could say good night in the hallway where others were present, then meet later in her room. As the relationship wore on, however, Little e became jealous of Jane and demanded of the relationship more than H. G. was willing to give. They argued and eventually parted. Years later they renewed their friendship.

Not long after the breakup with Little e, H. G. read some brilliantly composed articles by a writer who wrote under the name Rebecca West. Her real name was Cicily Fairfield. She had studied to be an actress and had adopted the name of Rebecca West as a stage name. After she grew disenchanted with life in the theater, she kept the stage name and used it in her writing career.

In one piece Rebecca called H. G. "pseudo-scientific." He contacted her and asked her to explain what she meant. They met for lunch at Easton Glebe. H. G. later said that she had "a curious mixture of maturity and infantilism about her....We argued and she stood up to my opinions very stoutly but very reasonably. I had never met anything quite like her before, and I doubt if there ever was anything like her before. Or ever will be again."

Rebecca was twenty-one and H. G. forty-seven when they met, but there was an immediate attraction between them. The relationship quickly grew closer as they visited each other several times. Then one day, while standing among his rows of books, they kissed. Rebecca declared her love for him at that moment and they became lovers. They had to meet secretly because her mother and sisters, whom she lived with, were against the affair. Soon Rebecca was pregnant and H. G. found a nearby house for her. He spent as much time with her as possible.

After Rebecca became pregnant the relationship grew more volatile. Her relatives tried to cover up the pregnancy. Rebecca was torn between being a rebel and defying society with her out-of-wedlock pregnancy, and being a proper middle-class British woman. "We did at times love each other very much," H. G. recalled, but they often argued. She wanted marriage and was jealous of Jane.

Rebecca and H. G. were different as writers. Rebecca was lively and vivid and unplanned. She wrote quickly when inspired. He was more methodical. He advised her to work out a scheme for her novel; she told him he was wasting his time on his nonfiction when he could be creating real literature. Their different approaches to writing became another source of friction. As time went on the couple argued more frequently. But there was a strong tie holding them together. For ten years H. G. split his time between Rebecca and their son Anthony (who later wrote a book about his famous parents) and Jane and his two sons.

When World War I broke out H. G. began to take assignments as a war correspondent. Work as a correspondent during the war kept him away a good share of the time.

World War I surprised most of the British people. H. G., however, had written extensively about the oncoming conflict. His 1908 scientific romance *The War in the Air,* had predicted the use of airplanes in modern warfare. In 1914 H. G.

Rebecca West and H. G. had one son together, Anthony, who later wrote a book about his parents.

published a series of newspaper articles on labor unrest and modern warfare that were later published in a book entitled *An Englishman Looks at the World.* In that same year he published his novel *The World Set Free*, which predicted the use of atomic bombs in a war with Germany. He had read about atomic theory and reasoned that degeneration of elements worked like the burning of coal, only more efficiently.

H. G. felt that the cause of World War I was that Germany had gone berserk. He thought this was the inevitable consequence of capitalist countries coming into conflict with each other in territorial struggles over less developed areas, such as Africa and Asia. He argued in newspaper articles that countries run by socialist governments could restore sanity to our planet because they would not be driven by profits to expand and grow empires.

At the beginning of the war H. G. saw an opportunity. He thought that the conflict between most of the leading western nations would end national identities. People would be so angry about the war that they would reach out across borders and find a peace that would defy the individual national governments. He published a pamphlet advocating his hope that this war would lead to a one-world government. He entitled the pamphlet "The War That Will End War." This phrase caught on and was used frequently. Later, American President Woodrow Wilson adopted the phrase when he was trying to convince the United States to enter the war in 1917.

Although he was initially convinced that World War I would result in world peace, H. G. was surprised that the war developed into such a destructive force and that it went on for such a long time. No one had ever seen war like this before. Even his fertile brain had never imagined such massive destruction. The horrible toll in lives and suffering was more than most people had predicted, and it soon became apparent that total victory would not be realized. This was not the war to end all wars. It was simply a seemingly endless, horrible bloodbath.

H. G. did not often volunteer his assistance in the war effort. He did, however, help in one matter. Tanks were being used for the first time, but they consistently got stuck in the mud. One evening while restlessly lying in bed, he had an idea. He jumped up and worked all night on a plan to solve the problem. His idea was to string wire between poles so the big machines could get traction. He presented his idea to Winston Churchill, who relayed the idea to the Ministry of Munitions. That department began to develop H. G.'s idea. The plans were finished before the end of the war, but military officers did not like the concept and it was dropped.

As the war dragged on, H. G. began to think the best solution was for the war to end. This growing opposition to the war was crystallized in one moment. He was walking in London to a meeting at his club when he noticed an ad on the wall of a building. The poster showed King George addressing a group that the king referred to as "my people." What struck H. G. was that there was no plural: the king did not say "our people." H. G. realized that Great Britain's monarchy was not just a harmless relic from the past, as he had thought before. It horrified him that a king still thought the millions were dying and suffering out of loyalty to an individual ruler. At that moment he also realized that "we were not making war against Germany; we were being ordered about in the King's war with Germany." H. G. concluded that his "war to end war" was something his imagination had created. As long as warring countries maintained and nurtured a ruling class, war would continue. H. G. elaborated his changed view of the war in the novel *Mr. Britling Sees It Through.*

H. G. continued to believe in the value of war in general. Armies would be needed to keep the peace. But he had lost confidence in this war. It proved difficult for him to publicly change his stance on the war. Some, on both sides of the issue, distrusted his sincerity.

H. G. also tried to use the war as a way to encourage lasting peace. One of his newspaper articles was published as part of the collection *What Is Coming?* in 1916, the year H. G. turned fifty. It argued for one-world government. "The realization of the imperative necessity of some great council or conference, some permanent overriding body, call it what you will, that will deal with things more broadly than any nationalism or patriotic imperialism can possibly do."

In 1917 the British government established a Ministry of Information. Lord Beaverbrook, an immensely wealthy owner of newspapers who was friendly toward H. G.'s ideas, was put in charge of this new office. A Ministry of Enemy Propaganda also came into being, run by Lord Northcliffe, another newspaperman who was friendly with Wells. Soon after taking his position in the propaganda office, Northcliffe asked H. G. to head an important committee. Wells agreed; he intended to use the office for peace propaganda, instead of as a way to issue war lies encouraging the citizens of England and confusing the Germans. His plans included a statement of war aims, which included the aim of peace. His committee prepared such a statement and submitted it to the Foreign Office. When that office rejected the document, H. G. resigned from his position.

At the end of the war President Wilson and other leaders of the Allies proposed an international organization should be formed. The idea was that the League of Nations would give world nations a place to discuss their differences. Hopefully, this would increase understanding and help avoid stumbling into another horrible war.

H. G. had another idea. He thought the league could be a first step toward his favorite political idea—one-world government. He worked to create an effective League of Nations that would work toward removing the importance of individual nations. He wrote several articles advocating his ideas. Not many people read them when they were published in the magazine *New Republic*. But when assembled into a 1918 book entitled *The Fourth Year,* readership increased. H. G. worked diligently, speaking and writing on behalf of the league. He was disillusioned, however, when his suggestions for how the league should be organized went unheeded. One of his ideas was for individual nations to submit to the decisions made by the league. This meant that national governments would be subservient to the league. H. G. wanted to end the individual nation-state and replace it with a one-world government. When it became clear that the league had no intention of following such a radical scheme, he lost confidence in the group's effectiveness. It became another in a long list of political disappointments for H. G.

H. G. was bitterly disappointed by the League of Nations. In his frustration he embarked upon an ambitious task. He wanted to write history in a way that would motivate people toward one-world government. The resulting book, *The Outline of History* (1920), sold extremely well in both the U.S. and Great Britain.

The Outline finally made H. G. a wealthy man. An abridged version, *A Short History of the World* (1922) also sold well. He later followed these books with *The Science of Life* (1931), about biology and *The Work, Wealth and Happiness of Mankind* (1932), about social sciences, including economics. H. G. referred to the social sciences as "Human Ecology."

Working on the books sapped his energy. He looked haggard and drawn and was frequently drowsy. At one point he came down with the flu and took a long time to recover. The cold English winters bothered his lungs. Fortunately, the success of *The Outline* enabled him to spend winters in southern France.

When the war ended, H. G. was disgusted by all the celebrating and the pomp and ceremony. He would rather have mourned the millions dead. He was bitter that so many had died and so little had changed. The one bright spot was

Russia, where Lenin and his small of group of communists, called the Bolsheviks, had seized power in 1917. He hoped that Lenin could carry through on his promises to bring a utopian worker state to giant Russia. In 1920 H. G. visited Russia, where he interviewed Lenin and other leaders of the new communist government. He also met with the writer Maxim Gorky. Out of that visit came a collection of his newspaper articles, *Russia in the Shadows* (1920).

During the war H. G. had tried to spend half his time at home with Jane and the boys, the other half with Rebecca and Anthony in London. After the war, however, Rebecca insisted on marriage or separation. Their relationship continued to be turbulent for several years. Finally, in 1923, Wells told Rebecca she should either break off their relationship or get serious about her own writing. This criticism stung. In October 1923 Rebecca left for a speaking tour in the United States. While there, she became more independent and developed a life of her own. When she returned to London, the relationship was over. They had grown apart, each with separate interests. H. G. still mourned losing her from his life. In his novel *The Secret Places of the Heart*, H. G. based the character Martin on Rebecca.

In April or May 1923, an Austrian woman visited London. She wrote to H. G. and asked to speak with him about the political situation in her country. At tea with the Wellses, the attractive woman described how educated people were persecuted in Austria. She also asked if she could translate one of H. G.'s books into German. He agreed.

The next time she came to the Wells residence, Jane was away. Without wasting much time, she declared her love for H. G. They began an affair, but she cared more for him than he did for her. She wrote steamy love letters. He tried unsuccessfully to end the relationship. He began refusing her phone calls. Dressing for dinner one night, he turned around to find her standing in the room. She announced, "You must love me, or I will kill myself. I have poison. I have a razor."

In a panic, H. G. had the maid phone for the hall porter. Meanwhile, the woman took out a razor and cut her wrists and armpits. He wrestled the razor from her hands, then tried applying cold water to stop the bleeding. "Let me die," she cried in a loud voice. "I love him. I love him."

The hall porter called for the police, who took her away to a hospital. H. G. went back to face a room full of blood. He called an influential friend, who contacted newspaper editors and asked that press coverage be stopped. Except for a brief mention in the tabloids, his incident went unnoticed.

Publicly, Jane supported her husband's desire for extramarital affairs and their resultant open marriage. Privately, she began retreating from their life together. Shortly after World War I she rented her own apartment and increasingly spent time there to work on her own writing.

For a brief period after the war H. G. became more involved in politics. He actively supported the Labour Party because he thought they might be likely to implement socialist ideas. He even ran for Parliament as a Labour Party candidate. Although he lost the race, he used the opportunity to spread his message. By 1924, however, he had lost faith in the ability of the Labour Party to implement reform. It seemed that H. G. could not be content in any political organization.

H. G. met the birth control and women's rights activist Margaret Sanger in 1920. In 1921, Wells was in Washington for a disarmament conference. He and Sanger were able to spend a week in New York together. Sanger remembered him as "amusing, witty, sarcastic, brilliant, flirtatious, and yet profound at once. He is quick, sensitive, alert to the slightest meaning, or intonation, or feeling."

In 1922 the Wellses planned a reception for various delegates attending a London conference on birth control. Margaret Sanger attended with her new husband, J. N. H. Slee. They had an arrangement similar to that between Jane and H. G. Wells and Sanger spent time together whenever they could.

After Rebecca West had gone her way in 1923, H. G. was haunted by memories of their time together. The relationship had lasted ten years. Then, during a visit to Geneva, Switzerland, in 1924, H. G. met Odette Keun. The relationship that developed helped him to recover from the pain of the breakup with Rebecca West.

Odette Keun was highly vain and emotionally unstable. But she had an affectionate side that attracted H. G. She could also make him laugh. "I did not fall in love with Odette, " H. G. reflected, "though I found her exciting and attractive. I thought only of myself in the matter. My life was restless and incomplete. I wanted, hidden away in the sunshine, a home to which I could retreat from England and work in peace. I wanted someone to keep house for me—and I wanted a mistress to tranquilize me and companion me."

They rented a house in the south of France, where H. G. planned to spend summers. They lived cheaply, even walking everywhere to keep from buying a car. Alone, the two got along well. But when they entertained others, Odette argued with H. G. in front of the guests or cut him off when he was talking. This left him angry and exasperated. Despite Odette's erratic behavior, he enjoyed the mild climate of southern France and managed to complete a considerable amount of writing. He enjoyed the arrangement enough that he had a home built for them in their favorite area "with bathrooms and a good kitchen, a garage, visitors' rooms...on a very pictur-esque bit of land with a big mass of rock and torrent and some good trees." The home was completed in 1927.

F. W. Sanderson was headmaster at Oundle School, where both Gip and Frank attended in Easton Glebe. He was a modern thinker and pioneer educator, who attempted to implement in the classroom what H. G. molded into theory. In his last days at Oundle, he was establishing what he called the House of Vision, a museum of history. It would have been a practical application of H. G.'s ideas.

H. G. believed that a better educational system could improve the world. As early as 1915 two organizations, the Committee on the Neglect of Science and the British Science Guild, were lobbying for more science study in schools, including more laboratory experience for students. H. G. was influential in their efforts. After the war, H. G. and Sanderson

Women's rights activist Margaret Sanger met H. G. in 1920.

worked to get more science into the schools. They felt it was time for classical education to make room for the new material. Their campaign resulted in no major changes, however. H. G.'s 1918 novel *Joan and Peter* deals with the educational situation at this time.

Unfortunately, Sanderson did not live to complete the task he had started with H. G. After the headmaster's sudden death by heart failure while speaking on the same speaking platform with H. G., Wells wrote *The Story of a Great Schoolmaster* (1924), a biographical tribute. When Sanderson's reforms were not continued by the new headmaster at Oundle, H. G. commented, "If...that House of Vision stands, misused and abortive, at Oundle, it is only like some gun that has been hit by a shell on the road to victory."

H. G. was attempting to make a difference in the world through his ideas. In his autobiography, he compared himself to Roger Bacon, who did similar work only to have it ignored until years after his death. Bacon, who lived from about 1214 till about 1292, was a philosopher and scientist with a special interest in optics. He too had to give up teaching because of ill health and had tried to develop a system of all knowledge. Eventually he criticized the Christian religion, a dangerous undertaking because he was a Franciscan monk. He was sent to prison.

H. G. was willing to admit that, like Bacon's ideas, his own would go unappreciated for a long time. He only hoped that someday they would be tested. He wrote: "The thoughts of Roger Bacon were like a dream that comes before dawn and is almost forgotten again. The sleeper turns over and sleeps on. All that Roger Bacon wrote was like humanity talking in its sleep. What is happening now is by comparison an awakening."

H. G. occasionally felt the need to flee from intellectual conflict. At various points he felt trapped. Then he had to get away to regroup and begin again. In 1924, H. G. effectively moved himself away from the controversy by traveling first to Switzerland and then to southern France.

In 1926, H. G. published *The World of William Clissold,* a three-volume novel centering on philosophy and personal relations. This was a major undertaking. Unlike many of his other novels, which developed at a brisk pace, this one came only after a considerable amount of waiting and writing and revising. It was a novel of ideas, not of events. One character was based on Odette Keun. Critics have questioned whether this book is fiction, autobiography, or philosophy—or a mix of all three.

Chapter Six

Losses and Gains

In January 1927, H. G. was sixty-one. He was spending the winter months living in southern France with Odette when he was suddenly called back to London. Jane, who was living in England and helping their younger son, Gip, prepare for his wedding, had been diagnosed with cancer. The doctors gave her about six months to live. Jane wanted to live long enough to see her younger son married, but she died the day before the wedding.

In keeping with her wishes, Jane's body was cremated. During the memorial service, H. G. watched her coffin go through the doors to the furnace room. "The coffin was pushed slowly into the chamber and then in a moment or so a fringe of tongues of flame began to dance along its further edges and spread very rapidly. Then in another second the whole coffin was pouring out white fire. The doors of the furnace closed slowly upon that incandescence."

H. G. and Jane had remained married for almost thirty-five years. While it had not been a typical marriage, it had been grounded in a mutual intellectual respect. Reflecting later, H. G. recognized three roles that his wife had played in his life. One was Jane, his wife and helper. A second was Catherine, the quiet writer. The third was "Mummy," the mother of their children. She played all three roles to perfection.

Back in France after Jane's memorial service, H. G. became entangled in more elaborate building and gardening plans at his home there. To add to his stress Odette began insisting that he marry her and reside in France full-time. H. G. wanted her to stick to the arrangement they had. "She was to leave me England and I was to give her France." Odette was not happy with this arrangement, and their relationship began to suffer.

The British Broadcasting Company wanted him to do radio talks. He had stubbornly refused their entreaties before. Finally, in 1929, he agreed to read excerpts from an address he had given previously in Germany. But he would not allow any censoring of his work. The studio provided a dinner beforehand and allowed him to pick his studio audience. He emphasized his usual theme—the need to let go of some national sovereignty in order to obtain world peace. Many complaints came in about the broadcast from people who thought that the station was broadcasting socialist propaganda. Newspaper and magazine reviewers were much kinder to H. G. Despite his raspy voice, the experience seemed to be a success. He agreed to further performances. After his second appearance, he received over 200 letters. The BBC continued to use him as guest speaker.

Three years after Jane's death, one of H. G.'s best friends, Arnold Bennett, died. By now most of the people who had visited the Wells residences on those colorful weekends were gone. Likewise, Joseph Conrad and Henry James, who had been both friends and foes over the years, had passed on. H. G. began to feel lonely.

By the end of the 1920s several silent films had been based on his works. With the advent of sound films at the end of the decade his novels *Things to Come*, *The Island of Dr. Moreau*, and *The Man Who Could Work Miracles* were made into movies.

In 1932, Aldous Huxley published his novel *Brave New World*. It was written to refute the points made in H. G.'s novel *Men Like Gods*. Aldous was the grandson of T. H. Huxley, Wells's biology teacher at South Kensington. In his work Wells had made the state nobler than the individual. He thought this was a positive thing. Huxley feared a society in which the state was more powerful than the individual.

Between 1928 and 1930, H. G. completed *Mr. Bletsworthy on Rampole Island* (1928), *The Autocracy of Mr. Parham* (1930), and *The Bulpington of Blup* (1932). All three books dealt with the role of the individual in conflict with collective action for world peace and world government. He was also spending a great deal of time in international speaking engagements. He was aware that he was addressing a world that had been through the horrors of World War I. But the world was rapidly changing. The Nazis were coming to power in Germany. Japan was in the grips of its military. The fascists under Mussolini had seized control of Italy. The type of capitalism practiced in England and the United States seemed to be losing ground to dictatorships. Hope for a long period of peace that had followed the end of World War I was disappearing. Free press, inexpensive newspapers, and wireless radio, tools that had seemed to offer more freedom of expression, were now being used as propaganda tools by the new dictators.

The new international organizations that H. G. had held out so much hope for during the war were now almost totally ineffective. By 1936 a newspaper poll of readers showed that forty percent had no faith in the League of Nations to stop future wars. Almost thirty percent wanted Britain to withdraw from the league. One commentator about the period observed, "Everywhere one looked the horrors were mounting, and nothing seemed possible to prevent them."

In 1931, when he was sixty-five, H. G. was out of energy. He knew something was wrong. A doctor discovered that he had diabetes. It was a mild case that could be controlled without daily insulin shots. As the treatment progressed H. G. felt some of his energy return. He wanted to return to England. The Mediterranean life was too easy going. He wanted to be in the middle of the hustle and bustle of London. May 22, 1933, was his last day of living in the south of France. He spent most of that day saying good-bye to his favorite black cat.

One of the reasons he wanted to leave France was that his relationship with Odette was ending. She had continued to insist he marry her and take her to England as his wife. Meanwhile, H. G. had met another woman. He had first met Moura Budberg when he visited Russia in 1920. She was his translator. She was physically appealing, often untidy, with a worried "forehead and a broken nose. . .with streaks of grey in her dark hair; she is a little inclined to be heavy physically; she eats very fast, taking enormous mouthfuls; she drinks a great deal of vodka and brandy without any manifest results, and she has a broad soft voice flattened perhaps by excessive cigarette-smoking." But she was charming and he was attracted to her. She had an air of self-confidence, calm but sure.

In March 1934, H. G. received an invitation to spend time in New York writing about President Franklin Roosevelt's New Deal for *Collier's* magazine. He also wanted to find out about filmmaking. He wanted to learn more about Hollywood's techniques on this visit.

He jumped at an opportunity to interview Stalin, the new leader of the Soviet Union. The USSR and the West were suspicious of each other. Because he was a supporter of socialism, H. G. was in a position to act as a mediator between the new communist country and the West.

Surprisingly, H. G. wanted to marry Moura. She preferred a steady but less formal relationship. As time went on it became clear that there was a mysterious side to her. When they traveled together she maintained secret telephone or telegraph ties to London or Russia. He began to realize that their relationship was only one part of her complex life. She was connected to various journalists and diplomats. In 1934, after she refused to accompany him on a visit with Stalin, H. G. discovered that she had been there shortly before his arrival— and had visited three times in the past year. He felt astounded, mystified, and betrayed. Why the deception?

Although H. G. wanted to marry the mysterious Moura Budberg, he came to realize that she was not to be trusted.

After the Russian trip, H. G. confronted Moura with what he had learned. Her only response was to deny his accusations. A deep distrust developed between them. They continued to see each other, but the bad feelings persisted. Eventually, H. G. came to the conclusion that, although he cared for her deeply, there was a limit to her devotion to him. He realized there was a deceitful side to her that he could never explain away.

But he did not want their relationship to end. She was now his most precious friend. In his autobiography he observed, "I can no more escape from her smile and her voice, her flashes of gallantry and the charm of her endearments, than I can escape from my diabetes or my emphysematous lung. My pancreas has not been all that it should be; nor has Moura. That does not alter the fact that both are parts of myself. " He decided, "In all my life I think I have really loved only three women steadfastly; my first wife [Isabel], my second wife [Jane], and Moura Budberg."

Partly as an effort to deal with his personal troubles, in May 1935, at age sixty-nine, H. G. began a book project he entitled *The Anatomy of Frustration*. He worked on it through the summer and fall and on into April 1936. *The Anatomy of Frustration* dealt with the war H. G. thought was approaching. He was frustrated that a new world ethic had not developed. Socialism had failed to provide this ethic and in this new work he provided a plan for attaining one-world government. He summarized the procedure this way: "The Frustration of World Peace...is due to the inadequate education of the human imagination and it can be defeated only by an immense poetic

In 1934, H. G. travelled to New York City to write for *Collier's* magazine.

effort, by teaching, literature, suggestion and illumination. A vast [battleground] lies between mankind and peace. We must go through that battle; there is no way round."

H. G. had an educational strategy to use in his overall reform plan. The first item on his agenda was a revision of school curricula, including introduction of science courses to lessen emphasis on the classics. The second item in his plan was to write three textbooks for self-education. They were *The Outline of History*, *The Science of Life*, and *The Work, Wealth, and Happiness of Mankind*. To effect a more direct reform he would have to make personal appearances. Between 1937 and 1939 he traveled extensively to promote the message set out in *The Anatomy of Frustration*. Part of the talk he gave on campuses was to push for a world encyclopedia. Aware that the worsening world situation was overtaking the remedies he advocated, he worked desperately to spread his views in time.

Chapter Seven

Defiant to the End

In February 1936, when H. G. was seventy, a film version of his novel *The Shape of Things to Come* (shortened to *Things to Come*) opened in London. It was successful commercially, but H. G. was disappointed. He felt that the entire production was mishandled. The next film was *The Man Who Could Work Miracles*. H. G. judged this to be an improvement over *Things to Come*.

In November 1938, H. G. traveled to Canberra, Australia, to attend the meeting of the Australia and New Zealand Associations for the Advancement of Science. During the visit he continued to find a way to create controversy. He spoke out against humanity's careless disregard of the planet Earth. At one point he said:

> What spendthrift ancestors we have had! What wastrels we still are! And all because history teaches us no better. Man burns and cuts down forests, he destroys soil, he acclimatizes destructive animals. A map of the world showing the devastated regions, where devastation is due to mankind, would amaze most people. It ought to be put

in every child's atlas.... If the young Hercules of a new
world is to live, its first feat must be to strangle the tangled
coil of poisonous old histories in its cradle.

Some critics thought that H. G. was overly optimistic
regarding the benefits of science. Others thought he had
turned into a pessimist. He saw nationalism as the enemy of
world peace. He said it "was the purest artificiality, and is
made by the teaching of history and nothing else, history
taught by parents, friends, flags, ceremonies as well as by the
persistent pressure of the schools, but mainly in the schools."
He feared, correctly, that intense nationalism was pushing the
world toward another war.

His worse premonitions came true when Germany invaded
Poland in September 1939. Soon the other European nations
were at war. London was being bombed almost nightly. H. G.
refused to move out of his home at 13 Hanover Terrace. His
attitude was one of bitter resentment. He had warned for
decades of this coming conflagration. No one had listened.
Now the bombs were falling and he refused to flee the terror.
What was the use? When the house across from him was
demolished, he marched outside and placed a larger "13" on
the front of his house, defying superstition.

H. G. had much to say when other countries entered the
war. This came out in several works, including *The Fate of
Homo sapiens*, *The New World Order*, *Travels of a Republican Radical in Search of Hot Water*, *The Rights of Man*, *The
Common Sense of War and Peace*, *Babes in a Darkling Wood*,

and *All Aboard for Ararat*. During the war he wrote three novels, three commentaries, fifty journalistic pieces, and three personal essays. He always seemed produce the greatest quantity of work during periods of great stress: the early 1890s, a time of personal domestic confusion and career uncertainty; World War I; and World War II.

In September 1940, despite the fact that the Atlantic was the scene of almost daily German attacks on British ships, seventy-four-year-old H. G. sailed for the United States. He was scheduled to deliver thirteen lectures. He went to New York, San Francisco, Connecticut, Florida, Texas, Alabama, Michigan, and Ohio. His speech emphasized the need for a common peace strategy to be devised by the three nations leading the allied side: Great Britain, the U.S., and the USSR. He argued against an anti-USSR bias among the American people. H. G. arrived back in London in January 1941.

H. G. was frustrated that his writings and lectures were having no effect on the war. When asked what he would like as an epitaph on his tombstone, he said: "Goddamn You All, I Told You So!" He saw few signs that people were willing to change.

He became increasingly harsh in his criticism of Great Britain and the other Allies during World War II. In his autobiography he announced, "I doubt if I shall live to see the end of this silly monarchy; this lying religious organization; this foul educational swindle; this tangle of snobbery and overreaching; that has been my inescapable background. I have jeered at it; I have laughed at it; maybe I have done something to hasten its end."

He felt that he was reaching the end of his life:

> My job of rebellion, which began when I was born, is now
> fully achieved and done. My mother's diary records that
> I squalled with extreme violence at the [baptismal] font.
> I would like to imagine I struck at the parson with my
> puny fist, but there is no proper evidence for that. My
> mute demand, "What is this lie of a world you have
> brought me into?" has taken me nearly seventy-six years
> to answer....

Despite his foreboding of approaching death, he continued
to write. In his last revision of *A Short History of the World*
(1944), he added a chapter called "Mind at the End of Its
Tether." The theme of this chapter was that humanity was
doomed, mainly because its nations had not learned to give
up sovereignty and agreed to live under one-world government. H. G. expanded "Mind at the End of Its Tether" into a
book-length work with the same title. In addition, he wrote
a much more positive book, *The Happy Turning*. He published
an article in an influential journal called the *New Leader*, in
which he pointed an accusing finger at people who would not
accept change. His friend J. B. Priestley wrote, "Of all the
English writers I have known, [Wells] was the most honest,
the frankest, the one least afraid of telling the truth. If he has
often offended public opinion, that is chiefly because English
public opinion feeds itself with cant and humbug."

During the war, and at the age of seventy-six, H. G. decided
to attend London University and earn a graduate degree in

zoology. He thought if he earned a doctorate, the highest degree, he might be admitted to the Royal Society, Great Britain's supreme organization of scientists. His dissertation was entitled "On the Quality of Illusion in the Continuity of the Individual Life in the Higher Metazoa, with Particular Reference to the Species *Homo sapiens.*" He argued that individuals do not have separate identity. Only collective enterprises would enable humans to live together in peace.

London University bestowed the degree of Doctor of Science on its famous elderly student. But the Royal Society refused to invite him to join. In the course of his long and controversial career he had angered too many influential people to gain admission into one of the bastions of the conservative, hierarchical society he complained about so loudly.

H. G. renewed his friendship with Beatrice Webb. He also restarted his correspondence with Elizabeth Healey, whom he had not written to regularly since the 1930s. In these last years he attempted a reunion with all his children. He desperately wanted them to get along and to approve of him. The only one who held back and could not accept her birth father was Anna-Jane, Amber Reeves's daughter.

On the afternoon of August 13, 1946, H. G. Wells died in his sleep. He was alone. His body was cremated three days later, and Gip Wells and Anthony West took his ashes out to sea

H. G. Wells was a "critic of progress." He believed the universe is hostile to human life, yet, human "progress" is the biggest threat to our existence. Wells had lived his life as he described it to his friend Elizabeth Healey in 1888: "Things were given for me to pitch stones at. Sometimes I fancy that is what gives me my profoundest pleasure—to chuck things at things and break them."

This man who rejected biblical truth was heralded as a prophet at his death. His accounts of air war and atomic war are terribly relevant today. His "radical" pronouncements on gender liberation have come to seem commonplace. Many of his educational ideas are practiced in schools. His views on ecology and environmentalism were several decades ahead of their time. Even still, one of his most cherished ideas has not come to pass—one-world government.

Wells clung to his conviction that literature for its own sake, for the sake of "art," was not as important as literature that conveyed a message or instructed. One of H. G.'s literary heroes was Jonathan Swift, who had freely mixed social criticism with artistic work. Like Swift, H. G. could not forsake putting a social message into his work.

It is as the father of modern science fiction, however, that most people remember him. This was not what H. G. wanted. He considered himself a great thinker on social issues. But his scientific romances, written early in his career before he became a public figure, still seem vital and relevant in today's world. In addition, they are fun to read and promise to attract generation after generation of bright young readers for decades to come.

Annotated Bibliography

H. G.'s *A Modern Utopia* (1905) is not just a utopian novel; it became his pronouncement on sex and morality. *In the Days of the Comet* (1906) explores jealousy as a motivating force in love relationships. *Ann Veronica* (1909) paints a picture of the truly liberated woman. Other books dealt with this theme as well: *Anticipations* (1900), *The New Machiavelli* (1911), *Marriage* (1912), *Passionate Friends* (1913), and *The Wife of Sir Isaac Harman* (1914). Three books—*The Secret Places of the Heart* (1922), *Meanwhile* (1927), and *The World of William Clisshold* (1926)—explored how a woman can be a good citizen without allowing society to destroy her.

When the Sleeper Awakes (1898), made fun of so-called scientific progress as seen in major modern cities of the world. He developed similar themes in *A Story of the Days to Come* (1899) and *A Dream of Armageddon* (1903). In *The Food of the Gods* (1904) H. G. explored how scientific achievement might be monitored and controlled.

In *The Food of the Gods* H. G. transformed his approach to the scientific novel, and began writing futuristic fiction. In this book, bungling scientists create a new food that can produce giants. The experiment gets out of hand, with disastrous results. Some of his finest action-writing describes a doctor's escape from giant rats.

Futuristic fiction first attracted young people to his books.

A Modern Utopia expanded on H. G.'s hopes for mankind in the future. He was working on the practical tasks of creating the "New Republic." He divided citizens into four classes—"the poietic, the kinetic, the dull and the base." The poietic citizens were the ones with vision, those who would legislate and lead. The kinetic would carry out the designs set by the poietic ones. The dull could always strive to join the ranks of the kinetic ones. The base were the mentally ill and the criminal element, beyond help and in need of separation from the rest. In fact, anyone except the base could strive to become a member of the Samurai, the top group of visionaries who would undertake political and social change. For a while he struggled to make the Fabian Society become the instrument that would help turn society toward this four-tiered class system.

Both *Ann Veronica* and *The New Machiavelli* outraged the church and other members of the status quo. This naturally made more young people enthusiastic about reading the controversial author. The main character in *Ann Veronica* talked and acted just like Amber Reeves, one of H. G.'s early lovers. Reviewers strongly criticized the amoral tone of the book. H. G. was even pressured to resign from one of his favorite organizations, the London Club.

The New Machiavelli attempted a fictional version of the debate he had instigated within the Fabian Society. It was so controversial that its publisher, Macmillan, delayed publication. Two characters treated somewhat negatively in the story were obviously modeled on Sidney and Beatrice Webb, leaders of the Fabian Society. The book created a scandal because of the inclusion of sexual suggestions, and H. G. became dismayed by the turmoil. At a later time, he reflected, "It is only by giving from his own life and feeling that a writer gives life to a character. Writers are like God in this at least, that they make men into their own image and their own breath gives them such life as they have."

H. G. created a vision of how he thought life could be. *First and Last Things* (1908) gave a personal statement of belief and *The Great State* (1912) provided a definition of socialism. H. G. believed that a person had to put his self-interests secondary to the interests of the group.Therefore, the individual could seek realization through the state. H. G. did not support communism, rather a democratic form of socialism based on his theories of science and philosophy.

Timeline

1866   Born September 21 in Bromley, Kent.

1874-9 Broken leg; studies at Morley's Academy, Bromley.

1879-82 Apprenticeships.

1883-4 At Midhurst Grammar School as pupil and pupil-teacher.

1884-7 At Normal School (later Royal College) of Science, South Kensington; edits *Science Schools Journal.*

1887-8 Teaches at Holt Academy, North Wales; injury and illness.

1888-9 Teaches at Henley House School, Kilburn; marries Isabel Wells; earns Bachelor's of Science degree.

1890   Tutor at Correspondence College.

1892   Meets Amy Catherine Robbins; publishes journalism.

1894-5 Divorces Isabel and marries Amy Catherine Robbins.

1898   Ill again.

1900   Builds Spade House, Sandgate, Kent.

1901   G. P. ("Gip") Wells born.

1903-4 Frank Wells born; joins Fabian Society.

1906-7 First visit to America; relationships with Rosamund Bland and Amber Reeves; break with Fabians.

1909   Birth of Amber Reeves's and H. G.'s daughter, Anna-Jane.

1911   Move to Easton Glebe.

1913   Meets Rebecca West.

1914   First visit to Russia; outbreak of WWI; son with Rebecca West born.

1916   Tours battle fronts in France, Germany, and northern Italy.

1918   Works with Ministries of Information and Propaganda; on League of Nations committee.

1920   Visits Russia; interview with Lenin; meets Moura Budberg.

1921-2 Covers World Disarmament Conference, Washington, for newspaper; relationship with Margaret Sanger; runs for Parliament unsuccessfully; renews connection with Webbs and Labour Party.

1923-4 Ends relationship with Rebecca West; meets Odette Keun.

1927 Amy Catherine "Jane" Wells dies.

1928 First talks in worldwide campaign for peace.

1930 Moves to apartment in Chiltern Court, London.

1931 Break-up with Odette Keun.

1933 Begins relationship with Moura Budberg.

1934 Visits USSR and interviews Stalin; visits USA and interviews FDR.

1935 Moves to 13 Hanover Terrace, London.

1936 PEN (Poets, Essayists, and Novelists) dinner in honor of seventieth birthday; awarded Doctorate of Literature by University of London.

1937 Chairs Section L of British Association for the Advancement of Science.

1938-9 Visits Australia to attend Australian and New Zealand science convention; in Stockholm for PEN conference as WWII begins.

1940 Stays at Hanover Terrace throughout bombings; speaking tour of U.S.

1943-4 Awarded Doctorate of Science by University of London.

1946 Dies in August; memorial service in October.

Major Works

1888　"The Chronic Argonauts" in *Science Schools Journal*
1895　*The Time Machine, Select Conversations with an Uncle, The Wonderful Visit, The Stolen Bacillus and Other Incidents*
1896　*The Island of Dr. Moreau, The Wheels of Chance*
1897　*The Invisible Man, The Plattner Story and Others, Thirty Strange Stories, Certain Personal Matters, The Star* 1898, *The War of the Worlds*
1899　*When the Sleeper Awakes, Tales of Space and Time*
1900　*Love and Mr. Lewisham*
1901　*Anticipations, The First Men in the Moon, A Dream of Armageddon*
1902　*The Sea Lady, The Discovery of the Future*
1903　*Twelve Stories and a Dream, Mankind in the Making*
1904　*The Food of the Gods*
1905　*Kipps, A Modern Utopia*
1906　*In the Days of the Comet, Socialism and the Family, The Future in America, The Faults of the Fabians*
1908　*First and Last Things, The War in the Air, New Worlds for Old*
1909　*Tono-Bungay, Ann Veronica*
1910　*The History of Mr. Polly*
1911　*The New Machiavelli, The Country of the Blind and Other Stories*
1912　*Marriage, The Great State*
1913　*The Passionate Friends, Little Wars*
1914　*The Wife of Sir Isaac Harman, The World Set Free, The War That Will End War*
1915　*Boon, The Research Magnificent, Bealby*
1916　*Mr. Britling Sees It Through, The Elements of Reconstruction, What Is Coming?*
1917　*The Soul of a Bishop; War and the Future; God, the Invisible King*

1918   Joan and Peter, In the Fourth Year
1919   The Undying Fire, History is One, The Idea of a League of
        Nations
1920   The Outline of History, Russia in the Shadows
1921   The Salvaging of Civilization
1922   Washington and the Hope of Peace, A Short History of the
        World
1923   Men Like Gods, The Story of a Great Schoolmaster, The
        Dream, Socialism and the Scientific Motive
1924   A Year of Prophesying
1925   Christina Alberta's Father
1926   The World of William Clissold
1927   Meanwhile, Collected Short Stories, Democracy under Revi-
        sion, Collected H. G. Wells
1928   The Open Conspiracy, Blue Prints for a World Revolution, Mr.
        Blettsworthy on Rampole Island, The Way the World Is Going
1929   The Autocracy of Mr. Parham, film script for The King Who
        Was a King, The Common Sense of World Peace
1931   The Science of Life, What Are We to Do with Our Lives?
1932   The Bulpington of Blup; The Work, Wealth and Happiness of
        Mankind; After Democracy
1933   The Shape of Things to Come
1934   Experiment in Autobiography
1935   The Anatomy of Frustration, The Croquet Player, The Man
        Who Could Work Miracles
1938   Apropos of Delores, World Brain, The Brothers
1939   The Fate of Homo sapiens, Travels of a Republican in Search
        of Hot Water, The Holy Terror
1940   Commonsense of War and Peace, Babes in the Darkling Wood,
        All Aboard for Ararat, The Rights of Man, The New World
        Order, A Sample of Life 1901-51
1941   Guide to the New World, You Can't Be Too Careful
1942   Phoenix, Science and the World Mind, The Conquest of Time
        (revision of First and Last Things), The Outlook for Homo sapiens
1943   Crux Ansata
1944   '42 to '44: A Contemporary Memoir
1945   Mind at the End of Its Tether, The Happy Turning, The Betterave
        Papers

Glossary

abdomen	part of body between thorax (heart and lung area) and pelvis.
agate	fine-grained stone with colors arranged in stripes, clouds, or mosslike forms.
alienated	made unfriendly or hostile.
argonauts	adventurers engaged in a quest.
autocracy	government in which one person possesses unlimited power.
bowler	player that delivers the ball to the batsman in cricket.
burlesque	mockery or caricature; humorous theatrical entertainment.
callow	lacking adult sophistication; immature.
charisma	special magnetic charm or appeal.
chronic	marked by frequent occurrence.
cleft	divided.
corporal	physical, affecting the body.
cricket	game played with ball and bat by two sides of usually eleven players each on a large field centering upon two wickets, each defended by a batsman.
crockery	earthenware: ceramic ware made of slightly porous opaque clay fired at low heat.
curricula	courses offered by educational institutions; content and methods of those courses.

distension	quality of being stretched or swollen.
draper	dealer in cloth.
ethic	set of moral principles or values.
flux	change.
frugal	economical, thrifty.
havoc	wide and general destruction; great confusion and disorder.
indefatigable	untiring.
irascibility	trait making one quick to anger.
portentous	weighty or pompous (self-important).
posit	to pose as an explanation.
scapegoat	one bearing the blame for others.
sovereignty	supreme power; freedom from control.

Bibliography

Batchelor, John. 1985. *H. G. Wells*. New York: Cambridge University Press.

Costa, Richard Hauer. 1967. *H. G. Wells*. New York: Twayne Publishers.

Coren, Michael. 1993. *The Invisible Man: The Life and Liberties of H. G. Wells*. New York: Atheneum.

Foot, Michael. 1996. *H. G.: The History of Mr. Wells*. London: Black Swan.

Haining, Peter, ed. 1978. *The H. G. Wells Scrapbook*. London: Clarkson N. Potter.

Hammond, J.R., ed. 1980. *H. G. Wells: Interviews and Recollections*. Totowa, NJ: Barnes and Noble Books.

Kemp, Peter. 1982. *H. G. Wells and the Culminating Ape*. New York: St. Martin's Press.

Raknem, Ingvald. 1962. *H. G. Wells and His Critics*. Norway: Universitetsforlaget.

Smith, David C. 1986. *H. G. Wells: Desperately Mortal*. New Haven: Yale University Press.

Wells, G. P., ed. 1984. *H. G. Wells in Love: Postscript to An Experiment in Autobiography*. Boston: Little Brown and Co.

Wells, H. G. 1934. *Experiment in Autobiography*. New York: B. Lippincott Co.

West, Anthony. 1984. *H. G. Wells: Aspects of a Life*. New York: Random House.

West, Geoffrey. 1930. *H. G. Wells: A Sketch for a Portrait*. London: Gerald Howe Ltd.

Sources

CHAPTER ONE

p. 9 "...we used to draw..." West, Geoffrey. *H. G. Wells: A Sketch for a Portrait*. London. Gerald Howe Ltd., 1930, pp. 28-29.

p. 10 "miserable wobblers..." West, op. cit., pp. 28-29.

p. 10 "I do not remember any..." West, op. cit., pp. 28-29.

p. 16 "a little blue-eyed..." Wells, H. G. *Experiment in Autobiography*. New York: B. Lippincott Co., 1934, pp. 40-41.

p. 19 "We sleep 4 together..." Wells, op. cit., pp. 90-91.

p. 21 "What is Wells doing?" Wells, op. cit., pp. 118-119.

p. 21 "Get out of this..." Wells, op. cit., p. 121.

p. 22 "Might I not be..." Wells, op. cit., p. 122.

p. 22 "Puff and rumble..." Wells, op. cit., p. 124.

CHAPTER TWO

p. 23 "...a slight, fair youth..." West, op. cit., p. 44.

p. 23 "...an energetic capable..." West, op. cit., p. 43.

p. 24 "By *what right*..." Wells, op. cit., p. 141.

p. 24 "He was bald and..." Wells, op. cit., p. 141.

p. 25 "When I saw him so close..." West, op. cit., p. 49.

p. 25 "...was callow and cautious..." Coren, Michael. *The Invisible Man: The Life and Liberties of H. G. Wells*. New York: Atheneum, 1993, pp. 37-38.

p. 26 "...she had a grave and..." Wells, op. cit., p. 227.

p. 28 "Judd was a better teacher..." Wells, op. cit., p. 183.

p. 28 "[Microscopes] let me into..." Wells, op. cit., p. 186.

p. 32 "What is to become..." Wells, op. cit., p. 236.

p. 32 "I improvised lessons in..." Wells, op. cit., p. 241.

p. 33 "...a pretty girl..." Coren, op. cit., p. 43.

p. 34 "I began to observe and..." Wells, op. cit., p. 250.

p. 36 "Someday I shall..." Foot, Michael. *H. G.: The History of Mr. Wells*. London: Black Swan, 1996, p. 18.

p. 36 "I have a faint..." Foot, op. cit., p. 18.

p. 36 "I have been dying for..." Wells, op. cit., p. 254.

CHAPTER THREE

p. 38 "...a fragile figure..." Wells, op. cit., p. 299.

p. 39 "No more teaching..." Wells, op. cit., p. 304.

p. 40 "...parted in the..." Wells, op. cit., pp. 294-295.

p. 42 "And it was *you*..." Wells, op. cit., pp. 294-295.

p. 43 "...for years I had..." Wells, op. cit., p. 301.

p. 43 "...he emphasized his..." Wells, op. cit., p. 434.

CHAPTER FOUR

p. 46 "All life is imperfect..." Wells, op. cit., p. 389.

p. 48 "pomes" Wells, op. cit., p. 429.

p. 48 "picsuas" Wells, op. cit., p. 313.

p. 48 "...a man of genius..." Foot, op. cit., p. 29.

p. 59 "scientific and industrial progress" Wells, op. cit., p. 556.

p. 59 "political and social structures" Wells, op. cit., p. 556.

p. 59 "I was writing..." Wells, op. cit., p. 552.

p. 62 "And through all this..." Wells, G.P., ed., *H. G. Wells in Love: Postscript to an Experiment in Autobiography*. Boston: Little Brown and Co., 1984, p. 32.

p. 63 "...the deliberate direction..." Smith, David C. *H. G. Wells: Desperately Mortal*. New Haven: Yale University Press, 1986, p. 96.

CHAPTER FIVE

p. 65 "pseudo-scientific" Wells, op. cit., p. 94.

p. 65 "...a curious mixture..." Wells, op. cit., pp. 94-95.

p. 66 "We did at times..." Wells, op. cit., p. 98.

p. 69 "my people" Wells, op. cit., 571.

p. 70 "...we were not..." Wells, op. cit., p. 571.

p. 70 "The realization of the..." Wells, op. cit., p. 571.

p. 74 "You must love me..." Wells, op. cit., p. 105.

p. 75 "...amusing, witty..." Smith, op. cit., p. 404.

p. 75 "I did not fall..." Wells, op. cit., p. 125.

p. 76 "...with bathrooms and..." Wells, op. cit., p. 130.

p. 78 "If...that House of..." Wells, op. cit., p. 624.

p. 78 "The thoughts of ..." Wells, op. cit., p. 624.

CHAPTER SIX

p. 80 "the coffin was..." Wells, op. cit., p. 45.

p. 81 "Mummy" Wells, op. cit., p. 29.

p. 81 "She was to..." Wells, op. cit., p. 136.

p. 83 "Everywhere one looked..." Smith, op. cit., p. 307.

p. 84 "...forehead and..." Wells, G.P., op. cit., p. 136.

p. 86 "I can no more..." Wells, op. cit., p. 210.

p. 86 "In all my life..." Wells, op. cit., p. 60.

p. 86 "The Frustration of World Peace..." Smith, op. cit., p. 313.

CHAPTER SEVEN

p. 89 "What spendthrift..." Foot, op. cit., p. 258.

p. 91 "...was the purest..." Foot, op. cit. p. 257.

p. 91 "I doubt if..." Wells, G.P. op. cit., pp. 226-227.

p. 91 "My job of..." Wells, H. G., op. cit., p. 229.

p. 92 "Of all the ..." Foot, op. cit., p. 303.

p. 93 "critic of progress" Haining, Peter, ed., *The H. G. Wells Scrapbook*, Foreword.

p. 93 "Things were given for me..." West, op. cit., p. 52.

Index